Influential Women

Hillary Clinton

Craig E. Blohm

ReferencePoint Press®

San Diego, CA

© 2016 ReferencePoint Press, Inc.
Printed in the United States

For more information, contact:
ReferencePoint Press, Inc.
PO Box 27779
San Diego, CA 92198
www. ReferencePointPress.com

LIBRARY OF CONGRESS CATALOGING-IN-PUBLICATION DATA

Blohm, Craig E., 1948- author.
  Hillary Clinton / by Craig E. Blohm.
    pages cm. -- (Influential women)
  Includes bibliographical references and index.
  Audience: Grade 9 to 12.
  ISBN 978-1-60152-950-3 (hardback) -- ISBN 1-60152-950-3 (hardback) 1. Clinton, Hillary Rodham--Juvenile literature. 2. Presidents' spouses--United States--Biography--Juvenile literature. 3. Women cabinet officers--United States--Biography--Juvenile literature. 4. Cabinet officers--United States--Biography--Juvenile literature. 5. United States. Department of State--Biography--Juvenile literature. 6. Women legislators--United States--Biography--Juvenile literature. 7. Legislators--United States--Biography--Juvenile literature. 8. United States. Congress. Senate--Biography--Juvenile literature. 9. Women presidential candidates--United States--Biography--Juvenile literature. 10. Presidential candidates--United States--Biography--Juvenile literature. I. Title.
  E887.C55B55 2016
  327.730092--dc23
  [B]
                                                                2015026626

Contents

The Many Lives of Hillary Clinton

History textbooks are filled with stories of courageous Americans fighting for freedom and democracy, exploring strange and unknown places, and challenging the boundaries of science, technology, and physical endurance. For much of American history, these stories featured men exclusively. In the thirteen colonies and the new nation formed from them, only men could vote or hold office. Women have had to fight for their place as citizens, gaining the right to vote only after the passage of the Nineteenth Amendment to the Constitution in 1920.

Many women have overcome the culture of gender inequality to make important contributions to society. These contributions include numerous firsts. Belle Babb Mansfield became the first woman lawyer in America, passing the Iowa bar in 1869. In 1932 Hattie Caraway was the first woman to be elected to the US Senate. And in 1997 Madeleine Albright became the first woman appointed secretary of state of the United States. In the twenty-first century, one woman who had already become a lawyer, a senator, and a secretary of state sought to claim another first: the first female president of the United States. That woman was Hillary Rodham Clinton.

Hillary's Early Years

Born of middle-class parents in middle America, Hillary Rodham grew up in the 1950s, a time of peace and prosperity. She was a bright student who could never quite live up to her father's expectations of excellence. She recalls, "My father would come home and say, 'You did well, but could you do better? It's hard out there.'"[1] Hillary did not let the fact that she was a girl limit her potential. She worked hard in school and developed a keen sense of competitiveness.

As the comfortable fifties transformed into the turbulent sixties, Hillary also underwent a change. In 1962 she went to Chicago with her church youth group to hear a speech by Martin Luther King Jr. For the first time Hillary became aware of the problem of race in America. Her awareness of social causes grew throughout high school and college, as did her intellect, her idealism, and her ambition. After college she attended Yale Law School, where she met a student from Arkansas named Bill Clinton. They married in 1975 and moved to Little Rock, Arkansas, where she joined the prestigious Rose Law Firm and eventually became the firm's first woman partner.

> *"My father would come home and say, 'You did well, but could you do better? It's hard out there.'"*[1]
>
> — Hillary Clinton.

First Lady Hillary

Hillary was thrust into the world of politics when Bill was elected governor of Arkansas in 1978. In her role as First Lady of Arkansas, Hillary worked to improve health care for the poor and reform the state's educational system. In the middle of his fifth term as Arkansas governor, Bill was nominated as the Democratic candidate for president of the United States in 1992. Hillary was now in the national spotlight, and her personal and professional life came under intense public scrutiny. During the campaign, the press investigated investments Hillary had made while at Rose Law. Hints that Bill had engaged in extramarital affairs started appearing in tabloid newspapers. Hillary defended herself, and her husband, against those who tried to derail the Clinton campaign. Bill won the election, and Hillary became America's First Lady.

Controversy followed Hillary to the White House. During the campaign, Bill had promised Americans that "when you vote for Bill Clinton, you get two for the price of one,"[2] envisioning Hillary as his partner in the Oval Office. Once Bill was elected, however, many people became critical of Hillary's active role in the Clinton presidency. Her proposal for a new system of health care reform failed to win the support of Congress and was abandoned. The suicide of a

Hillary Clinton campaigns in New Hampshire in 2015. Clinton—former First Lady, former New York senator, and former secretary of state—hopes to add another title to her resume: President of the United States.

former Rose Law coworker, Bill's affair with a White House intern, and accounts of Hillary's often volatile temper all combined to tarnish her self-controlled public persona. Despite the vindictiveness of her detractors, however, Hillary actually gained sympathy for enduring Bill's indiscretions.

When the Clinton presidency ended in 2001, no one would have blamed Hillary if she had decided to put the world of politics far behind her. But her ambition would not allow her to retreat from public life.

Senator Clinton

That same year, Hillary Clinton became the first former First Lady to be elected to the US Senate. As a senator from New York, she helped citizens of her new home state in the aftermath of the September 11, 2001, attacks. She voted in favor of the US invasion of Iraq. She visited US troops in Iraq and Afghanistan, and she voted to help banks during the economic crisis of the late 2000s. With her rising popularity and increasing foreign policy experience, Clinton decided to take the ultimate step: a run for the presidency.

Clinton announced her candidacy in January 2007. During the primary campaign that would decide who the Democratic nominee for president would be, Clinton was opposed by several other candidates, among them Senator Barack Obama of Illinois. With the field finally narrowed down to Clinton and Obama, Clinton lost the nomination to the man who would become the nation's first African American president. Shortly after being elected, Obama asked Clinton to be his secretary of state, a position of global importance. Clinton accepted, and she began her new job on January 22, 2009. She served in the position until 2013.

> *"I'm running for president. . . . Everyday Americans need a champion. And I want to be that champion. So I'm hitting the road to earn your vote— because it's your time. And I hope you'll join me on this journey."*[3]
>
> —Hillary Clinton.

A Second Campaign

With her experience as a senator and secretary of state, Clinton once more decided to run for president. On April 12, 2015, she announced a new bid for the White House. In a two-minute video, she declared, "I'm running for president. . . . Everyday Americans need a champion. And I want to be that champion. So I'm hitting the road to earn your vote—because it's your time. And I hope you'll join me on this journey."[3] That journey, wherever it takes her, will be a historic one for Hillary Clinton and the capstone of her long and influential career in public service.

Chapter One

Hillary Growing Up

In 1961 the competition between the United States and the Soviet Union for the conquest of space was heating up. On April 12 Soviet cosmonaut Yuri Gagarin became the first human in outer space; less than a month later, the United States joined the space race as Alan Shepard roared into the sky. For America's youth, astronauts like Shepard became heroes rivaling sports figures and comic book superheroes. NASA, the US space agency, received thousands of letters from children wanting to become astronauts. One such letter was written by a fourteen-year-old girl named Hillary who dreamed of one day flying in space. Those dreams were dashed, however, when she received NASA's reply, which stated succinctly, "We are not accepting girls as astronauts."[4]

The rejection infuriated the young girl, but it did not discourage her from pursuing her dreams. By the time NASA began recruiting women for the astronaut corps in 1978, she was already on her way to making her own indelible mark on American history. For Hillary Rodham, the sky was definitely not the limit.

A Middle-American Youth

The years following World War II saw the United States gradually returning to a state of normalcy. Soldiers and sailors were coming home to start families and return to civilian employment. Hugh Rodham had spent the war in the US Navy, training recruits at a large training center near Chicago. After the war ended in 1945, he returned to the Chicago apartment where he and his wife, Dorothy, resumed a normal life. Hugh began a drapery business, and Dorothy continued her role as homemaker. Dorothy became pregnant, and on October 26, 1947, the Rodhams welcomed their first child, Hillary Diane, into their family.

Hugh Rodham's business prospered, and in 1950 he moved his family, which now included son Hugh, to the Chicago suburb of Park Ridge. It was a white, middle-class, middle-American town, one of the numerous suburbs nationwide where veterans settled down to raise the "baby boomer" generation. For the Rodhams, this included Hillary, Hugh, and eventually Tony, who was born in 1954. Park Ridge schools were good, the streets were safe, and there were plenty of children for Hillary to play with. Dorothy describes their neighborhood: "There must have been forty or fifty children within a four-block radius of our house and within four years of Hillary's age. They were all together, all the time, a big extended family. There were more boys than girls, lots of playing and competition. [Hillary] held her own at cops-and-robbers, hide-and-seek, chase-and-run—all the games that children don't play anymore."[5]

Astronaut Alan Shepard awaits launch into space in May 1961. Around this same time, a young Hillary Rodham wrote to NASA about her dream of becoming an astronaut. The space agency responded that it was not accepting girls into the program.

Dorothy Rodham's Challenging Life

The most influential woman in Hillary Clinton's life was her mother, Dorothy Rodham. Dorothy's own life, however, was one of struggle and hardship. She was born in Chicago in 1919 to teenage parents who divorced when she was eight years old. Dorothy and her younger sister were sent by train, alone, to live with their grandparents in California. Life there was miserable for the girls, who were tormented by their strict and cruel grandmother. As punishment for trick-or-treating one Halloween, Dorothy was confined to her room for a year during all but school hours.

At age fourteen Dorothy struck out on her own and was taken in by a family as their children's caretaker. There she learned what it was like to live in a caring household. After graduating from high school, Dorothy returned to Chicago to live with her mother, who had asked her to come home. Hoping to go to college, Dorothy soon found that her mother only wanted her for performing household chores. Feeling deceived, Dorothy moved out, rented an apartment, and got a job to support herself. In 1937 Dorothy met Hugh Rodham, and they were married five years later.

Despite a life of hardships, Dorothy Rodham was a skillful homemaker, loving mother, and a positive influence on her daughter. After Dorothy's death in 2011, Hillary reflected, "Mom measured her own life by how much she was able to help us and serve others."

Hillary Rodham Clinton, *Hard Choices*. New York: Simon & Schuster, 2014, p. 589.

Hillary was a tomboy at heart and, with her mother's encouragement, learned to stand up for herself. When a tough neighborhood girl named Suzy O'Callaghan began pushing Hillary around, her mother said, "If Suzy hits you, you have my permission to hit her back. You have to stand up for yourself. There's no room in this house for cowards."[6] Hillary took her mother's advice, and Suzy became one of Hillary's lasting friends.

A Demanding Father

Dorothy was the voice of encouragement in the Rodham family; Hugh was just the opposite. Demanding and opinionated, Hugh ran the household with an iron hand and a booming voice. A child of the Great Depression in the 1930s, Hugh was thrifty to the point of obsession. Hillary seldom got to buy new clothes, and winter nights at the Rodham house were frigid because Hugh turned the furnace off to save money. Most of the neighborhood children received allowances from their parents, but not the Rodham kids. "They eat and sleep for free," Hugh said. "We're not going to pay them for it as well."[7] Hugh's thrift did have its limits—he always drove an expensive and luxurious Cadillac.

Pleasing their father seemed impossible for Hillary, Hugh, and Tony. Hillary's grades in school, while excellent, never seemed to satisfy her father. If her report card had all As and one B, it was the lone B that Rodham focused on, chiding Hillary for not doing better. When she did get all As, his response was, "You must go to a pretty easy school."[8] Despite his gruff demeanor, Hugh was a devoted father, helping his children with their homework and playing board games with them. "He was a tough taskmaster," Hillary recalls in her autobiography, "but we knew he cared about us."[9]

> *"If Suzy hits you, you have my permission to hit her back. You have to stand up for yourself. There's no room in this house for cowards."*[6]
>
> —Dorothy Rodham, Hillary's mother.

School Days

Providing a good education was one way that Hugh showed he cared for his children. The good schools in Park Ridge were a major factor in Hugh's decision to move his family there. Eugene Field Elementary School was just a few blocks from the Rodham home, and Hillary walked there every day. She excelled in her class work, getting top grades and outpacing her brothers in academics. An enthusiastic athlete, she played soccer, softball, tennis, and other sports. As a Girl Scout, Hillary accumulated numerous merit badges, including several for community service. Scouting, Hillary remarked in a 2012 speech, taught her "life long lessons about leadership and the value of public service."[10]

At Eugene Field and later at Ralph Waldo Emerson Junior High, Hillary began to learn that not everyone was fortunate enough to live in a comfortable suburban environment. Not far from Park Ridge were many small farms employing seasonal migrant workers. During harvest season Hillary babysat for the youngest children of the migrant families so the older children could help their parents in the fields. Along with her neighborhood friends, she organized games, carnivals, and a mock Olympics, donating the proceeds to charity.

Entering Maine East High School in the fall of 1961, Hillary found the academic competition tougher than in grade school or junior high. She had to work harder than ever to make the honor roll, to the mild annoyance of her brother Hugh. "When she wasn't studying," he commented, "she was a lot of fun. But she was always studying."[11] Hillary's study habits did not interfere with her abundant extracurricular activities. Her yearbook senior profile included activities such as junior class vice president, school newspaper, Girl's Athletic Association, Cultural Values Committee, Speech Activities and Debate, Pep Club, and Variety Show. Hillary's relentless pursuit of being the best at everything caused some animosity among her peers, one of whom later expressed irritation with her overachieving classmate: "Hillary was so take-charge, so determined, so involved in every single activity that you'd think, 'Why don't you chill out a bit? Why don't you give somebody else a chance?' I always felt Hillary thought she knew what was best, so that's what everybody should do."[12]

> *"When she wasn't studying, she was a lot of fun. But she was always studying."*[11]
>
> —Hugh Rodham, Hillary's brother.

In high school Hillary was outgoing and made friends easily, at least among the girls. Many boys, however, seemed to be put off by her self-confidence, as well as by her less-than-stylish clothes, lack of makeup, and thick glasses. Hillary disliked wearing those glasses and often went without them during school. Many students came to regard Hillary as standoffish, since she sometimes ignored them as they passed in the hallways. In fact, she was so nearsighted that without her glasses, she did not recognize those who gave her a friendly greeting.

An Active Faith

School was only one of the nurturing influences on Hillary's life. The expression of faith was an integral part of Hillary's family life, as she recalls: "We talked with God, walked with God, ate, studied, and argued with God. Each night, we knelt by our beds to pray before we went to sleep."[13] Every Sunday the Rodhams attended the First United Methodist Church. Dorothy became a strong spiritual influence on Hillary, teaching Sunday school and demonstrating the Christian principles of prayer and service to others. Hillary responded by faithfully attending worship services, going to summer Bible school, and becoming involved in church-sponsored youth groups.

During her early high school years, a new influence entered her life, one that had a dramatic effect on her view of the world and her role in it. In the fall of 1961 a young man driving a shiny red Chevrolet convertible pulled up to First United. Reverend Donald Jones was a handsome twenty-six-year-old just out of divinity school. He had been hired as the church's new youth minister—and he was about to shake up the meaning of religion for the church youth.

A Maturing Social Conscience

Jones became a mentor to Hillary, not only spiritually but socially and politically as well. In his youth group, called the University of Life, he exposed the teens of the church to the world outside the confines of their sheltered neighborhood. He introduced the group to art house films, the writings of modern theologians, and Bob Dylan's music. Freewheeling discussions centered on diverse topics such as radical politics, teenage pregnancy, and the art of Pablo Picasso. Jones balanced his intellectual discussions with practical experiences by taking the group to visit black and Hispanic churches on Chicago's South Side. "Sitting around church basements," Hillary recalls, "I learned that, despite the obvious differences in our environments, these kids were more like me than I ever could have imagined."[14]

On a chilly night in April 1962, Jones took the group to hear Martin Luther King Jr. speak at Chicago's Orchestra Hall. At the time, Hillary's knowledge of the Civil Rights Movement was limited, but King's speech captivated her. Hillary listened attentively as

Martin Luther King Jr. speaks in Washington, DC, in August 1963. The previous year, Hillary's church youth group attended a King speech in Chicago. Hillary describes herself as being inspired by King's words.

King spoke eloquently of racial injustice, the poor, and the politics of conscience. "Until then," Hillary later recalled, "I had been dimly aware of the social revolution occurring in our country, but Dr. King's words illuminated the struggle taking place and challenged our indifference."[15] After the speech, Jones took the group backstage to personally meet King and shake his hand.

Introduction to Politics

King's speech inspired in Hillary a new social awareness, but several events in the early 1960s began to transform her emerging political views. America at midcentury had prospered under the administration of Republican president Dwight Eisenhower. Like most residents of Park Ridge, Hugh Rodham was, according to Hillary, "a rock-ribbed, up-by-your-bootstraps, conservative Republican and proud of it."[16]

Inspiring Words of Martin Luther King Jr.

Martin Luther King Jr. gave the speech "Remaining Awake Through a Great Revolution" numerous times throughout his life. The words that inspired Hillary also gave thousands of others a new understanding of race relations. The following is an excerpt from the speech, given by King on March 31, 1968, just four days before he was assassinated.

> It is an unhappy truth that racism is a way of life for the vast majority of white Americans, spoken and unspoken, acknowledged and denied, subtle and sometimes not so subtle—the disease of racism permeates and poisons a whole body politic. And I can see nothing more urgent than for America to work passionately and unrelentingly—to get rid of the disease of racism. . . .

> For more than two centuries our forebearers labored here without wages. They made cotton king, and they built the homes of their masters in the midst of the most humiliating and oppressive conditions. And yet out of a bottomless vitality they continued to grow and develop. If the inexpressible cruelties of slavery couldn't stop us, the opposition that we now face will surely fail.

> We're going to win our freedom because both the sacred heritage of our nation and the eternal will of the almighty God are embodied in our echoing demands. And so, however dark it is, however deep the angry feelings are, and however violent explosions are, I can still sing "We Shall Overcome."

Martin Luther King Jr., "Remaining Awake Through a Great Revolution," King Institute. http://kingencyclopedia.stanford.edu.

Under Hugh's influence, it was not surprising that Hillary embraced her father's political preference.

In the 1960 presidential election, Democrat John Kennedy defeated Richard Nixon by a narrow margin. The final tally was extraordinarily close: Kennedy had won by a mere 118,574 votes out of more than 68 million cast. Republicans suspected fraud among the voters of Cook County, Illinois, which was controlled by the powerful Democratic political machine of Chicago mayor Richard Daley. Hugh Rodham loudly expressed his outrage at the alleged cheating, but it was his thirteen-year-old daughter who took action. Hillary and a friend learned about a Republican group that was seeking volunteers to look into suspected voting irregularities in Chicago. Without telling their parents, the two teenagers took a bus to the city, where they were assigned separate areas to investigate. Hillary was driven to a poor neighborhood on the South Side and left alone to go door to door, checking residents against voter lists. She recalls:

> "I also felt sorry for our country and I wanted to help in some way, although I had no idea how."[18]
>
> —Hillary Clinton.

Off I went, fearless and stupid. I did find a vacant lot that was listed as the address for about a dozen alleged voters. I woke up a lot of people who stumbled to the door or yelled at me to go away. And I walked into a bar where men were drinking to ask if certain people on my list actually lived there. . . .

When I finished I stood on the corner waiting to be picked up, happy that I'd ferreted out proof of my father's contention that "Daley stole the election for Kennedy."[17]

Hillary's father was furious at her for such a risky escapade, conceding that, fraud or not, the outcome of the election was not going to be changed. Although Hillary remained a staunch Republican, she admired the young and energetic Kennedy's visionary outlook. On November 22, 1963, the nation and the world were shocked by Kennedy's assassination in Dallas, Texas. When Hillary got home from school that day, she found her mother glued to the television watching coverage of the assassination. Hillary remarked that as the nation mourned its slain leader, "I also felt sorry for our country and I wanted to help in some way, although I had no idea how."[18]

Hillary the Goldwater Girl

Despite her sorrow at Kennedy's death, Hillary was not quite ready to break free from her father's political influence. She continued to identify with the Republican Party, joining her school's Young Republican organization. Hillary's political stance was encouraged by her ninth-grade history teacher, Paul Carlson. Conservative and fiercely anti-Communist, Carlson's worldview was the polar opposite of Donald Jones's liberal outlook, stressing individual self-reliance over government involvement in social concerns. Carlson urged Hillary to read a book called *The Conscience of a Conservative* by Arizona Republican

Senator Barry Goldwater, the Republican nominee for president, campaigns in 1964. Hillary avidly supported Goldwater and worked for his campaign.

senator Barry Goldwater, a manifesto of the author's political philosophy of individual self-reliance and small government. After reading the book, Hillary wrote a term paper on American conservatism, dedicating it to her parents. When Goldwater ran for president against President Lyndon Johnson in 1964, Hillary campaigned for the senator. As one of the candidate's Goldwater Girls, she donned a cowgirl outfit, complete with a cowboy hat bearing the campaign logo "AuH$_2$0," the chemical symbols for gold and water.

By now Hillary had transferred from overcrowded Maine East to the newly opened Maine South High School for her senior year. With the election approaching, Jerry Baker, one of her new teachers, organized a mock debate between the presidential candidates. Hillary was surprised when she was chosen to play the liberal Johnson, while a liberal student represented the conservative Goldwater. Hillary studied diligently to prepare for her role. "I immersed myself—for the first time—in President Johnson's Democratic positions on civil rights, health care, poverty and foreign policy."[19] Students then held a mock election, which, despite Hillary's debating skills, was handily won by the Republican candidate.

In real life, Goldwater was not so fortunate: He was roundly defeated by the incumbent Johnson. While Goldwater's philosophy of rugged individualism still appealed to Hillary, the mock debate had given her a revealing look into the other side of the political spectrum.

A Constant Influence

During her elementary and high school years, Hillary had been influenced by many conflicting forces. Her father's strict perfectionism stood in stark contrast to her mother's quiet nurturing. The passionate liberalism of Jones ran squarely against the zealous conservatism of Carlson. But one influence that remained constant in Hillary's life was her Methodist faith and its teachings of compassion for others.

A famous rule for living, attributed to John Wesley, the eighteenth-century cofounder of Methodism, states: "Do all the good you can, by all the means you can, in all the ways you can, in all the places you can, at all the times you can, to all the people you can, as long as ever you can."[20] This precept would guide Hillary throughout her life in public service. In the meantime, though, her thoughts were focused on deciding which college to attend.

Chapter Two

Wellesley, Yale, and Bill Clinton

In the fall of 1964, many of Hillary's classmates had already decided on attending local colleges, and Hillary considered doing the same. Her guidance counselor, burdened with the pressures of advising a large group of new students, offered little help beyond handing her college brochures. However, two women who taught at Maine South that fall helped Hillary make her college choice. Janet Altman and Karin Fahlstrom were graduate students teaching government at the school while studying for their master's degrees at Northwestern University. Altman had graduated from Smith and Fahlstrom from Wellesley, both nationally recognized women's colleges located in Massachusetts.

Hillary had not considered going to an eastern college, but she kept an open mind. Her father worried about the influence that liberal East Coast schools would have on his daughter. Although Hillary had not thought about attending an all-women's institution, there would likely be some advantages to such a choice. A classmate told her, "You don't have the thing where women don't put their hands up because someone might not take you out because you know the answer and they don't."[21]

Hillary applied to Smith and Wellesley and was accepted at both. Never having visited either campus, she had to choose between the two. She based her decision on a photograph she saw of a lake on the Wellesley campus, which reminded her of the lake near her family's summer cottage. The idyllic campus scene clinched the deal: Hillary would go to Wellesley.

Welcome to Wellesley

With the family car packed with suitcases, Hugh, Dorothy, and Hillary began the thousand-mile (1,609 km) trip from Park Ridge to

Wellesley College, located just outside of Boston. Upon reaching their destination, Hillary bid her parents goodbye and headed for her new home in Wellesley's Gothic-style Stone-Davis dormitory.

"The thing I remember most were the conversations. She would rather sit around and talk about current events or politics or ideas than go bicycle riding or to a football game."[24]

—Geoffrey Shields, a friend of Hillary Clinton.

Hillary had been at the top of her class in high school, but at Wellesley she was just another inexperienced freshman. "I felt lonely, overwhelmed, and out of place,"[22] she recalls. The atmosphere at Wellesley was one of upper-class sophistication, filled with wealthy young women who had traveled abroad, had attended private boarding schools, and spoke foreign languages fluently. The culture shock Hillary experienced led her to consider leaving Wellesley and returning home. Her decision was acceptable to Hugh, but Dorothy convinced her to stay and tough it out. "After a shaky start," Hillary remembers, "the doubts faded, and I realized that I really couldn't go home again, so I might as well make a go of it."[23]

Changing Times

It was not long before Hillary began to fit in. She joined the Young Republican organization and was soon elected its president. Although most girls on campus were concerned with dating and other social activities, Hillary had more serious things on her mind. Geoffrey Shields, a Harvard student and friend of Hillary, recalls, "The thing I remember most were the conversations. She would rather sit around and talk about current events or politics or ideas than go bicycle riding or to a football game."[24] As Hillary's reputation grew, more students requested to live at Stone-Davis to be near her. The dorm's dining hall became a center for lively conversations led by Hillary.

The social upheaval that rocked the nation in the late 1960s played out most visibly on college campuses. Although still a Republican, Hillary was in the forefront of the change taking place at Wellesley. Classmate Diane Canning later described her as "quite active politically—even then—and very much a spokesperson for

An unnamed photographer captures an image of Hillary at Wellesley College in the 1960s. A wealthy student population and sophisticated atmosphere was a bit of culture shock for someone who grew up in a middle-class Chicago suburb.

change."[25] But she always advocated for change by working within the system. When violent protests for civil rights and against the Vietnam War began growing at colleges around the country, Hillary joined peaceful marches and criticized the violence displayed by student demonstrators on other campuses. Her disapproval of the

Republican stances on civil rights and Vietnam led her to resign as president of the Young Republicans.

As Hillary became more interested in the Civil Rights Movement, she decided that she should learn more about the lives of African Americans. In her freshman class of about four hundred students, there were only six black women, and Hillary made an effort to get to know them personally. "She was just a friend," remembers classmate Karen Williamson. "All the black students in our class felt we had a very close friendship in Hillary."[26]

One Sunday, Hillary invited Williamson to attend church with her. Not surprisingly, it caused quite a stir within the white Methodist congregation. When friends back in Park Ridge learned what Hillary had done, they expressed doubt about the wisdom of her exploit, deeming it merely a symbolic gesture. Hillary later said she had done it to test the church, but she went on to admit that she was testing herself as well. It was an education for Hillary to learn firsthand how society treated minorities.

A Religious Foundation

Attending church services nourished Hillary's spiritual life. Despite the changes she was going through at Wellesley, one constant was her deep-seated Methodist faith. Donald Jones, her mentor at First United Methodist in Park Ridge, continued to be Hillary's spiritual adviser. "The key to understanding Hillary," recalls Jones in a 1993 magazine article, "is her spiritual center. . . . Her social concern and her political thought rest on a spiritual foundation."[27] He corresponded with Hillary during her years at Wellesley, becoming a long-distance sounding-board as she began to grow and change, both politically and personally. In a 1966 letter to Jones, Hillary asked, "Can one be a mind conservative and a heart liberal?"[28] It was a concise description of Hillary in her early college career: following her father's conservative politics intellectually while having heartfelt compassion for the downtrodden.

Two Martyrs

On April 4, 1968, civil rights leader Martin Luther King Jr. was slain by an assassin at the Lorraine Motel in Memphis, Tennessee. Johanna Branson, Hillary's roommate at Wellesley, was sitting in their room, unaware of the shooting. She recalls Hillary's reaction. "Suddenly the door flew open. Her bookbag flew across the room and slammed into the wall. She was distraught. She was yelling. She kept asking questions. She said, 'I can't stand it anymore. I can't take it.' She was crying."[29]

The next day, as riots broke out in Detroit; Chicago; Washington, DC; and other cities, an anguished Hillary joined a protest march in Boston. "I returned to campus wearing a black armband," Hillary recalls, "and agonizing about the kind of future America faced."[30] The King tragedy sparked an episode of activism at Wellesley: The black student organization Ethos threatened a hunger strike if the college did not take steps to address the lack of minorities on campus. "Clearly, it was the first form of activism at the campus," recalls professor Stephen London. "I remember Hillary very vividly being supportive, really relating to that."[31] As the newly elected president of the student body, Hillary mediated between the protesters and administration to find a workable solution. In the end the college agreed to the group's demands and began recruiting more minority students and faculty.

> "The key to understanding Hillary is her spiritual center. . . . Her social concern and her political thought rest on a spiritual foundation."[27]
>
> —Donald Jones, professor.

Just two months later, Robert Kennedy, who was seeking the Democratic nomination for president, was assassinated while campaigning in Los Angeles. Home from college for the summer, Hillary learned the news from her mother. She spent the day talking on the phone to a friend about the future of America after the lives of two great men had been snuffed out by assassins' bullets. The deaths of King and Kennedy in the spring of 1968 were defining moments in the nation, as well as in Hillary's life. That summer she finally chose which side of the political fence she would stay on.

Washington, Miami, and Chicago

In the summer of 1968, Hillary was one of thirteen Wellesley women selected for a nine-week internship program in Washington, DC.

Hillary was assigned to the House Republican Conference, doing office work for Congressman Melvin Laird. Although she spent the summer within the Republican camp, she retained her growing Democratic leanings, especially concerning the war in Vietnam. "She presented her viewpoints very forcibly," Laird later recalled, "always had ideas, always defended what she had in mind."[32]

In early August, Hillary attended the Republican National Convention in Miami, working to support the nomination of moderate Republican Nelson Rockefeller. By the end of the convention, however, it was clear that Richard Nixon would become the party's nominee. Disappointed that Nixon, more conservative than Rockefeller, would represent the party in the November elections, Hillary finally acknowledged that the Republicans were headed in a direction she could not support. "I sometimes think that I didn't leave the Republican Party as much as it left me,"[33] she commented.

The Democratic National Convention began on August 26 in Chicago, and it was not going as smoothly as the Republican convention had. Some ten thousand protesters gathered at Grant Park in downtown Chicago to protest the Vietnam War. By the third night of the convention, television newscasts were filled with images of violent confrontations between demonstrators and the Chicago police. Hillary and her friend Betsy Johnson wanted to see the protests for themselves, so they drove downtown from Park Ridge. They were shocked by the sight, in Betsy's words, of "kids our age getting their heads beaten in. And the police were doing the beating."[34] Distressed by the violence at the convention, Hillary wondered if politics could ever change American society for the good.

Senior Year

With the sights and sounds of Chicago burned into her mind, Hillary returned to Wellesley in the fall of 1968 for her senior year. Along with attending classes and continuing her extracurricular activities, Hillary was faced with another decision: what should she do after college with

US soldiers conduct a search and destroy mission in Vietnam in 1967. Hillary was active in the Young Republicans organization while in college but gradually came to oppose US involvement in Vietnam.

a degree in political science? She considered working for Saul Alinsky, a radical community organizer from Chicago who offered to hire her after graduation. Hillary declined the offer, concluding that his approach to social change by radical activism clashed with her desire to effect change within the system. The best way to do that, she decided, was to attend law school.

Hillary's Alaskan Adventure

Hillary Clinton has accumulated vast experience in her jobs as a lawyer, senator, and secretary of state. But her most unusual job experience did not take place in the courtroom or the halls of Congress, but in the wilds of Alaska.

Clinton graduated from Wellesley in May 1969. Seeking a break from four years of study and student activities, she spent that summer working her way across Alaska. First she washed dishes at Mount McKinley National Park, then "slimed" fish at a salmon factory in Valdez. It was far from glamorous work, as Clinton recalls in her memoir, *Living History*.

> My job required me to wear knee-high boots and stand in bloody water while removing guts from the salmon with a spoon. When I didn't slime fast enough, the supervisors yelled at me to speed up. Then I was moved to the assembly packing line, where I helped pack salmon in boxes for shipping to the large processing plant offshore. I noticed that some of the fish looked bad. When I told the manager, he fired me and told me to come back the next afternoon to pick up my last check. When I showed up, the entire operation was gone. During a visit to Alaska when I was First Lady, I joked to an audience that of all the jobs I've had, sliming fish was pretty good preparation for life in Washington.

Hillary Rodham Clinton, *Living History*. New York: Simon & Schuster, 2003, pp. 42-43.

She applied to several law schools and was ultimately accepted by both Harvard and Yale. While deliberating about which school to choose, Hillary was invited to a Harvard Law School party. When she told a professor that she was having a hard time choosing between Harvard or its closest competitor, Yale, the man replied, "Well, first of all, we don't have any close competitors. Secondly, we don't need any more women."[35] With that remark, Hillary's decision was made: She would go to Yale.

Wellesley had never invited a student to speak at the commencement ceremonies, but when a group of students suggested the idea, student body president Hillary Rodham was the only logical choice. Her speech would follow an address by Republican senator Edward Brooke, the only black member of the Senate.

On graduation day, May 31, 1969, Brooke stepped to the platform on Wellesley's Academic Quadrangle. His speech turned out to be one of generalities, and Hillary thought it failed to address the real problems facing her generation. Brooke seemed to defend the Vietnam War and made no mention of the assassinations of Martin Luther King Jr. or Robert Kennedy. "The Senator," she recalled, "seemed out of touch with his audience: four hundred smart, aware, questioning young women."[36] When Brooke finished, Hillary stepped to the microphone. "I find myself," she declared, "reacting just briefly to some of the things that Senator Brooke said."[37] In her sometimes rambling speech, Hillary challenged Brooke's remarks by speaking out against the war and the excesses of corporate life in America, and reminding her classmates that the goal of education is human liberation, a freedom that must be realized in action.

> "Take a good look at her. She will probably be the president of the United States some day."[38]
>
> —Nancy Wanderer, a friend of Hillary Clinton.

At the conclusion of her speech, Hillary received a standing ovation from an audience that included her father, but not her mother, who was ill and unable to travel. Nancy Wanderer, a friend of Hillary attending the ceremony, turned to her mother and said, "Take a good look at her. She will probably be the president of the United States some day."[38]

Yale

Hillary entered Yale Law School in the fall of 1969, as one of 27 women out of a total of 235 incoming students. The media attention that her Wellesley commencement speech had generated paved the way for her to be perceived as a leader from the moment she set foot on the school's New Haven, Connecticut, campus. Classmate Patricia Coffin Fry remarked, "While there were other women committed to

An Advocate for Children

Marian Wright Edelman, founder of the Children's Defense Fund, inspired Hillary's lifelong activism on behalf of children. As noted by journalist Carl Bernstein, the two women shared social and spiritual outlooks.

Already Hillary regarded her as something of a hero for using the system, especially the courts, on behalf of children. . . . Marian embraced many of the same traditional values—self-reliance, family, hard work, equal justice, universal brotherhood, the pursuit of knowledge—that Hillary had so tenaciously held on to through the turbulence of the 1960s. She and Edelman shared a religious interpretation of social and political responsibility. Edelman, like Hillary, was fond of proverbial language and aphorisms: "You really can change the world if you care enough." "Service is what life is all about." "Children don't vote, but adults who do must stand up and vote for them." The words could have just as easily rolled from Hillary's lips. Like the advocate Hillary would become, Marian also was focused, determined, winsome, and, if necessary, took no prisoners as she marched toward an imperative objective.

Carl Bernstein, *A Woman in Charge: The Life of Hillary Rodham Clinton.* New York: Knopf, 2007, p. 71.

public service, Hillary just stood out as someone who was marching forward."[39]

During her first year Hillary continued to apply herself to her studies as she had in high school and college, while debating social issues with fellow students after class. She was invited to join the Youth Advisory Committee of the League of Women Voters, a national civic affairs organization. On May 7, 1970, Hillary spoke at the fiftieth anniversary convention of the league in Washington, DC. The keynote speaker at the convention was Marian Wright Edelman, a Yale Law School graduate and an advocate for children's rights. Hillary was struck by how similar Edelman's views on helping the disadvantaged were to her own. When Edelman spoke later that spring at Yale, Hillary asked her if she could work for her during the summer. Edelman offered her a job but could not pay her. Hillary received a grant to pay her expenses and spent the summer researching the health and education of the children of migrant workers for Senate committee hearings in Washington, DC. That summer convinced Hillary that her future lay in using the law to help underprivileged families and children.

Meeting Bill

In the spring of 1971, Hillary was studying in the Yale library when she noticed a young man with reddish hair and beard staring at her. She had seen him around campus before, but the two had never met.

Bill Clinton and Hillary Rodham (photographed during their college years) met while both were attending Yale University Law School. Despite their initial attraction to each other, they went their separate ways for a time.

This time, however, Hillary took the initiative. She went over to the man and said, "If you're going to keep looking at me, and I'm going to keep looking back, we might as well be introduced. I'm Hillary Rodham."[40] It took a flustered Bill Clinton several seconds to respond with his own name.

Hillary already had a boyfriend, but something about the bearded young man kept her interested, and by that summer they had become a couple. When classes began in the fall, they rented an apartment in New Haven. Alike in intellect but different in temperament, the two complemented each other. According to historian William H. Chafe, "Bill was gentle, affable, averse to conflict, and loath to attack other people. Hillary was tough, direct, willing to fight and take the battle to the other side."[41]

Although Hillary had entered Yale a year earlier than Bill, she spent an extra year studying at the Yale Child Study Center, so they graduated together in the spring of 1973. On a trip to Europe that summer, Bill proposed to Hillary. Certain that she loved him but not sure that she could make such a permanent commitment, Hillary turned him down. Although they did not officially break up, they went their separate ways. Hillary was unsure of what the future held for her, but Bill knew what he wanted. "I'm goin' back to Arkansas," he said, "and I'm going to be governor."[42]

With Bill heading south, Hillary decided to put her law degree to work in her field of interest: children's rights. She moved to Cambridge, Massachusetts, to work as a lawyer for the Children's Defense Fund, an advocacy group. While there, her legal research projects ranged from investigating prison conditions of incarcerated teenagers to comparing school enrollment figures with census records to determine how many children were not attending school. In the meantime, Bill took up a teaching position at the University of Arkansas in Fayetteville and began preparing for his political career. He hoped that, in time, Hillary would join him.

Chapter Three

First Lady Hillary

Hillary's new job at the Children's Defense Fund was an exciting and fulfilling experience for the twenty-six-year-old Yale graduate. Hillary loved the work, but she missed Bill. She decided to accept an offer to join the faculty at the University of Arkansas where Bill was teaching. Hillary packed her bags and headed south, where "I had the time and space to give our relationship—and Arkansas—a chance."[43]

Marrying Bill

She arrived in Fayetteville in August 1974, in the midst of Bill's campaign for a seat in the US House of Representatives. Bill campaigned hard against his Republican opponent, John Paul Hammerschmidt. Hillary worked in his campaign headquarters—writing speeches, advising Bill, and even selling sandwiches to raise money for the campaign. She kept the campaign on a moral high ground when she refused to allow it to accept money from a dairy industry source that would have expected political favors in return.

When the final votes were tallied on Election Day, Bill lost by about six thousand votes. His defeat depressed him, and he says he spent the next several weeks at Hillary's house "nursing my regrets and trying to figure out how I was going to pay off my campaign debts."[44] His depression eventually lifted, and both he and Hillary taught spring courses at the University of Arkansas. After the semester ended, Hillary took a trip to the East Coast, and when she returned, Bill had a surprise for her. "Remember that little house you liked so much?" he asked, referring to a small brick home she had once admired. "I bought it. You have to marry me now, because I can't live there alone."[45] They were married in the house on October 11, 1975, surrounded by family and close friends.

On to Little Rock

After Bill's loss in the election, another move was in store for the Clintons. Still pursuing a political career, Bill ran unopposed for the office of Arkansas attorney general and was elected in 1976. The Clintons moved to the state capital of Little Rock, where Hillary sought to continue her law career. Vince Foster, an old friend of Bill, was a partner at the Rose Law Firm, an influential and politically active law practice in Little Rock. At the time, Rose Law had no women lawyers. Foster thought that should change, and he championed Hillary for a position at the firm. Hillary joined Rose Law in February 1977.

At Rose, Hillary concentrated on intellectual property law, a legal specialty dealing with protecting copyrights and trademarks in music, film, literature, and other artistic endeavors. But she also performed free legal work on cases involving children's rights. Being the only woman lawyer at the firm had disadvantages. Gossip about her appearance circulated among the office's secretaries. Hillary had never cared much for fashion, and she was mocked for her wardrobe and

After Bill and Hillary married, they settled in Little Rock, Arkansas (pictured). Bill pursued a career in politics and Hillary continued with her law career, joining the prestigious Rose Law Firm.

attempts to look like a career woman. "There wasn't one stereotypically womanly or feminine thing about her,"[46] commented her own secretary. Such criticism would continue for years as she moved more and more into the public spotlight.

First Lady of Arkansas

Public criticism of Hillary intersected with Bill's political ambitions. In 1978 Bill began campaigning for governor of Arkansas. Although Hillary's job at Rose Law kept her busy, she helped out by advising her husband and evaluating his speeches. At campaign events, the two projected the image of a power couple ready to run the state together. However, many voters were uncomfortable with the idea that a governor's spouse would have a hand in running the state. They felt that political wives should limit their activities to social functions. Even the idea of a governor's wife having her own career troubled many voters.

Much of the disapproval centered on Hillary's name. After she married Bill, Hillary kept her maiden name instead of changing her name to Clinton. She did this to retain a sense of independence and also to prevent questions about any perceived conflict of interest with her husband's political career. But this did not go over well in a conservative state like Arkansas. Hillary inspired strong feelings among the people, both in Arkansas and elsewhere: They either loved her or hated her. Journalist Carl Bernstein notes, "Hillary was seen by many as a polarizing figure. For the first time, she became the object of intense dislike and verbal abuse."[47]

> "Hillary was seen by many as a polarizing figure. For the first time, she became the object of intense dislike and verbal abuse."[47]
>
> —Journalist Carl Bernstein.

Despite the public's love-hate affair with Hillary, Bill was elected governor of Arkansas on November 7, 1978. Hillary not only kept her job at Rose Law but advanced her position there. In 1979, at a time when partners in law firms were nearly always male, Hillary became the firm's first woman partner. Bill also found a place for his wife in his new administration. He appointed Hillary as chair of the Arkansas Rural Health Advisory Committee, which worked to improve health care in the vast rural areas of Arkansas.

In the midst of their busy lives and thriving careers, Bill and Hillary were also planning to start a family. That dream would be fulfilled in 1980, a year that presented the Clintons with both joy and disappointment.

A Challenging Year

Chelsea Victoria Clinton was born on February 27, 1980. The Clintons were overjoyed at being parents, but the birth again raised the issue of Hillary's decision to keep her maiden name. There was little doubt that Chelsea would bear the Clinton name, but some critics even began to question the legality of their marriage. Despite the continuing controversy, Hillary says she continued to use the name Rodham as a sign that she was "a person in my own right."[48]

The year 1980 was also an election year, and Bill was confident he would be reelected for a second term as governor. But Arkansas voters had other ideas, and at the end of election night, Bill lost by some 32,400 votes out of almost 839,000 cast. As with his loss in the House of Representatives election in 1974, Bill was devastated. In the months that followed his defeat, Hillary became a driving force behind Bill's recovery from depression. William H. Chafe writes, "He desperately needed Hillary to be his cocaptain, to steer the ship, to deliver unwelcome news, to balance his optimism with her realism."[49]

Back in the Governor's Mansion

Once out of office, Bill took a job at a Little Rock law firm while Hillary continued her work at Rose Law. But according to Dick Morris, Hillary's friend and coworker, Bill "was clearly not a happy man."[50] He thrived on being in the spotlight and holding public office; he spent the next two years preparing for another run at the governor's job. Knowing that public perceptions of Hillary had been an issue during Bill's first term as governor, she set about to change her image. By the time Bill's next campaign was underway in 1982, Hillary had adopted a completely new look. Her frumpy clothes gave way to tailored outfits, and her huge glasses were replaced by contact lenses. Her dark hair had been lightened and cut into a more flattering style. Most importantly, in a show of support for her husband, she began using Clinton as her last name.

Chelsea Clinton, pictured here with her parents in 1991, was born in 1980. The year she was born, her father lost his bid for a second term as Arkansas governor. Hillary was key to helping Bill out of a depression resulting from the loss.

The "new" Hillary played an even larger role in Bill's campaign than she had in 1978. She managed his schedule and traveled the state with Chelsea in tow, talking to voters on her husband's behalf. With her help, Bill handily defeated his opponent, and the Clintons moved back into the Arkansas governor's mansion in January 1983. An important campaign promise Bill had made was to improve the state's educational system, one of the worst in the nation. He created the Arkansas Education Standards Committee and appointed Hillary as its head. She traveled across the state, gathering data and listening to the concerns of parents, teachers, and school administrators. The committee's final recommendations included limited class sizes, a lengthened school year, and competency tests for teachers. Teachers balked at this last provision, considering being tested an insult to their competence. In addition, the tax increase necessary to fund the program was unpopular. Nevertheless, the committee's proposals became law, due in large part to Hillary's dedication as chair of the committee.

Bill would be reelected three more times, serving as Arkansas governor until 1992. By then he had his eyes on a bigger prize: the presidency of the United States.

On the Campaign Trail Again

On October 3, 1991, Bill announced his candidacy for president of the United States. As with his previous campaigns in Arkansas, Hillary became Bill's partner and adviser. On the campaign trail, Bill even advocated the idea of Hillary having a role in his administration, joking, "When you think of Hillary, think of our real slogan, 'Buy one, get one free!'"[51] But before the Clintons could dream about packing for Washington, they would have to answer some serious questions being asked by the press.

> *"When you think of Hillary, think of our real slogan, 'Buy one, get one free!'"[51]*
>
> —Bill Clinton.

Rumors of Bill's affairs had first cropped up during his campaign for the Arkansas House of Representatives. Now that he was running for president, the examination of his personal life intensified. Hillary admitted that they "were unprepared for the hardball politics and relentless scrutiny that comes with a run for the Presidency."[52] In a January 1992 tabloid newspaper story, a woman named Gennifer Flowers claimed to have had a twelve-year affair with Bill. Soon other media outlets picked up the story, and the scandal threatened to doom the campaign almost before it began.

Campaign advisers recommended that the Clintons refute the allegations, so on January 26 Bill and Hillary appeared on the CBS news show *60 Minutes*. Bill admitted that their marriage, like most, had good and bad times, and then Hillary commented:

> You know, I'm not sitting here, some little woman standing by her man like Tammy Wynette. I'm here because I love him and I respect him and I honor what he's been through and what we've been through together. And, you know, if that's not enough for people, then heck, don't vote for him.[53]

The television interview neutralized the accusations and convinced the voters that the issues, not Bill's personal life, were what

Hillaryland

Although it sounds like the name of an amusement park, Hillaryland was the nickname of Hillary's staff of campaign advisers during Bill's 1992 presidential run. It was unusual for a candidate's spouse to have her own staff, but the Clintons were not against flouting convention when they thought it was called for. The name *Hillaryland* was coined by a campaign aide on the spur of the moment when answering a telephone call at campaign headquarters in Little Rock, Arkansas. The whimsical name stuck, and soon a Hillaryland sign appeared on a wall at headquarters.

Hillaryland became a code word for allegiance to Hillary, a subculture consisting of her loyalists. It was at once a tight-knit circle of aides, a center of campaign strategy, and a refuge where she could go to be among friends when the stresses of campaigning became too great. Among the nearly all female Hillaryland staff were several women who would follow Hillary in her future political undertakings, including Patti Solis Doyle, who managed Hillary's Senate campaign and 2008 presidential run, and Huma Abedin, Hillary's longtime personal aide and vice chair of her 2016 presidential campaign. Hillaryland has evolved into a powerful political force. "Today," say journalists Jeff Gerth and Don Van Natta Jr., "no active political organization can match its depth, discipline, or devotion, according to Senate aides and political analysts." Such power may propel Clinton into the highest office in the land.

Jeff Gerth and Don Van Natta Jr., *Her Way: The Hopes and Ambitions of Hillary Rodham Clinton.* New York: Little, Brown, 2007, p. 217.

mattered. Hillary, however, was in for more criticism. Her comment about Tammy Wynette was seen as an attack on the country singer, not a reference to her popular song "Stand by Your Man." Hillary apologized to Wynette, but soon another public statement added to her troubles. When asked about a possible conflict of interest when Hillary worked at Rose Law while Bill was Arkansas governor, she said she "could have stayed home and baked cookies and held teas"[54] but instead chose to pursue a law career. Many saw the remark as an

The Clintons stop at a restaurant in Manchester, New Hampshire, during the 1992 presidential campaign. Hillary served as Bill's partner and adviser on the campaign trail.

affront to women who chose to stay home and raise families. Again, Hillary had to apologize.

On Election Day, November 3, 1992, Bill defeated his Republican opponent, incumbent George H.W. Bush. Bill had reached the goal of his long-held political ambitions. Hillary was also eager to make her mark on the national scene.

First Lady of the United States

The Clintons settled into the White House and immediately got to work. The most important item on the new president's agenda was overhauling the nation's health care system. "The greatest of their goals," explains Bernstein, "was to establish a system of universal health care in which every American would be insured against catastrophic illness and guaranteed adequate, paid lifelong medical care."[55] To accomplish this task, the National Health Care Reform Task Force was established with Hillary as its head.

Hillary consulted with experts in various areas of health care, chaired meetings of the task force, struggled with budget issues, and appeared before Congress. John LaFalce, congressman from New York, in commenting on her testimony, was impressed by "not just her grasp of facts, but her understanding of who is for and against what. . . . She doesn't put on any airs, there's no phoniness."[56] She conducted the task force's meetings in closed sessions in an effort to prevent undue influence from the media and industry groups. In doing so, Hillary alienated the medical, pharmaceutical, and insurance establishments, the industries with the most at stake in health care reform. Republicans also opposed the idea of universal health care, characterizing it as an intrusion of big government into the lives of Americans. Ads attacking the plan appeared nightly on television. Ultimately, the criticism was too much to overcome, and by September 1994 the Clinton health care reform plan was dead. Hillary was discouraged, admitting that "I knew that I had contributed to our failure, both because of my own missteps and because I underestimated the resistance I would meet as a First Lady with a policy mission."[57]

Emerging Scandals

Losing the fight for health care was a personal disappointment for Hillary, but worse was yet to come. Beginning in 1993 critics questioned the legality of the Clintons' involvement in a real estate venture known as Whitewater during Bill's tenure as governor of Arkansas. The investigation would continue into Bill's second term as president, although it eventually found no evidence of wrongdoing by either of the Clintons.

Hillary was also accused of improperly firing seven staff members of the White House travel office in order to replace them with Clinton friends. An investigation of her role in the so-called Travelgate scandal revealed that although she had made false statements to investigators about the travel office firings, there was not enough evidence to prosecute her.

In the midst of all these scandals, several personal tragedies rocked Hillary's life. In March 1993 her father died from a massive stroke; four months later Vince Foster, Hillary's close friend and colleague at Rose Law, committed suicide. Bill's mother, Virginia, died of cancer in January 1994. The first four years of the Clinton presidency were full of political turmoil and personal heartbreak. With hopes of better times, the Clintons looked forward to another term in the White House.

Second Term Affords a Second Chance

Bill Clinton was sworn in for his second term as president on January 20, 1997. The Clintons had not given up on improving health care, and this time their focus was on children. Hillary worked with both Democratic and Republican legislators to establish the State Children's Health Insurance Program, which provided health care coverage for millions of children. She was a critical link between legislators and the president in getting the legislation passed. Senator Ted Kennedy, a Democratic sponsor of the program, said in 2007, "The children's health program wouldn't be in existence today if we didn't have Hillary pushing for it from the other end of Pennsylvania Avenue."[58]

Hillary wanted to share her ideas on families in a way that would reach the public directly. The result was her first book, *It Takes a Village*, published in 1996. The title—attributed to an old African proverb—became a popular phrase in support of society's role in raising children. *It Takes a Village* spent more than twenty weeks on the *New York Times* best-seller list. Hillary donated her royalties from the book to charity.

During Bill's second term, Hillary continued a series of visits to foreign nations that she had begun in 1995. Speaking on behalf of children's and women's rights, Hillary traveled to some eighty countries, making her the most-traveled First Lady in US history.

The Lewinsky Scandal

Even with Hillary's extensive travels, she could not escape the consequences of her husband's affairs. In January 1998 news stories reported that a young White House intern named Monica Lewinsky had been engaged in an affair with President Clinton from 1995 to 1997 and that he tried to cover it up. Bill denied the reports, defiantly stating in a nationally televised news conference, "I did not have sexual relations with that woman, Miss Lewinsky. I never told anybody to lie, not a single time—never. These allegations are false."[59]

Hillary confronted Bill, and at first she believed his vow of innocence, calling the scandal part of a "vast right-wing conspiracy." She

The First Lady Visits China

After the failure of her health care initiative and the harsh criticism that its opponents directed at her, Hillary Clinton began to keep a lower public profile. But she was far from idle, traveling the world as a representative of the United States and speaking on behalf of women's and children's rights.

In September 1995 Clinton flew to Beijing, China, to speak at the United Nations Fourth World Conference on Women. There was much criticism of the conference, both domestically and abroad, due to China's history of human rights abuses. But Clinton's purpose was clear. "I want to push the envelope as far as I can on behalf of women and girls." Stepping up to the podium to deliver her address, Clinton looked out over the multiethnic audience and spoke from her heart.

> I believe that on the eve of a new millennium, it is time to break our silence. It is time for us to say here in Beijing, and the world to hear, that it is no longer acceptable to discuss women's rights as separate from human rights. . . . For too long, the history of women has been a history of silence. Even today, there are those who are trying to silence our words. . . . If there is one message that echoes forth from this conference, let it be that human rights are women's rights . . . and women's rights are human rights, once and for all.

Hillary Rodham Clinton, *Living History*. New York: Simon & Schuster, 2003, pp. 302, 305.

added that "the best thing to do in these cases is just to be patient, take a deep breath and the truth will come out."[60] The truth did come out, but not the way Hillary had hoped. As independent counsel Kenneth Starr, who was already investigating Whitewater, began probing the Lewinsky matter, Bill's denials fell apart, and he admitted to the affair.

Hillary was distraught and so angry with Bill that she barely spoke to him. But she ultimately found strength in her religious faith. After an uneasy ten-day vacation on Martha's Vineyard in Massachusetts in August 1998, the Clinton marriage was beginning to heal. Although the American public seemed to forgive Bill's infidelities, the Republican-led Congress was not ready to do the same. Articles of impeachment were issued by the House in December 1998, charging the president with lying under oath and obstructing justice in the Lewinsky affair. After a three-week trial in 1999, the president was acquitted of any misconduct.

Leaving the White House

The eight years of successes and scandals, triumphs and tragedies that made up the Clinton administration ended on January 20, 2001, when Republican George W. Bush took the oath of office as the next president. As the time to leave the White House approached, Hillary later wrote that she "wandered from room to room taking mental snapshots of all my favorite things in the White House . . . trying to recapture the wonder I felt when I first arrived."[61] Although an important chapter of Hillary's life was ending, she had already begun writing the next one.

Chapter Four

Senator Clinton

In November 1998 Hillary Clinton received a late-night telephone call from Charles Rangel, a Democratic congressman from New York and friend of the Clintons. Rangel had some news that he thought would interest the First Lady. "I just heard," he said, "that Senator Moynihan announced he is going to retire. I sure hope you'll consider running because I think you could win." Daniel Patrick Moynihan was a respected senator from New York; he had been in office since 1977. "I'm honored you would think of me," Clinton replied, "but I'm not interested, and besides, we have a few other outstanding matters to resolve right now."[62] Those matters were the ongoing Whitewater investigation and the Monica Lewinsky scandal.

Despite her reluctance to run for Moynihan's seat in the Senate, Clinton had already been thinking about her life after the president's term ended. Once they returned to Arkansas, she could resume her law practice or perhaps run a nonprofit organization or even become president of a college. In the abstract, a run for the Senate also sounded appealing. As early as 1997, a friend told Clinton that she would make a good senator. Other acquaintances also seemed confident that Clinton could win the Senate seat in New York. But Clinton had never lived in New York and was unsure if an outsider could win.

Listening to the People

A poll conducted in the spring of 1999 showed that many New York residents believed that Clinton should run. Out of this early indication of support came Clinton's "Listening Tour" of New York's sixty-two counties. As someone who was born in Illinois and had lived a good portion of her life in Arkansas, Clinton needed to familiarize herself with the issues facing New Yorkers and offset the fact that she was an outsider. "I think I have some real work to do," Clinton said, "to get out and listen and learn from the people of New York and demonstrate that what I'm for is maybe as important, if not more important, than where I'm from."[63] Clinton kicked off her tour on July 7 at Moynihan's farm in upstate New York, where she announced the formation of her Exploratory Committee for the US Senate. Clinton approached the microphone, wearing what would become one of her trademarks: a black pantsuit. Moynihan, whose seat she was seeking, stood next to her and declared, "I think she's going to win."[64]

Throughout the summer of 1999, Clinton traveled the state in a Ford conversion van jokingly dubbed the "HRC Speedwagon" by the press. But her tour was serious business, as Clinton relates in her autobiography.

> I stopped at diners and cafes along the road, just as Bill and I had done during his campaigns. Even if only a handful of people were inside, I'd sit down, have a cup of coffee and talk about whatever topics were on their minds. Campaign professionals call this "retail politics," but to me, it was the best way to stay in touch with people's everyday concerns.[65]

With her blue Ford conversion van in the background, Hillary Clinton greets New Yorkers during her statewide tour in the summer of 1999. Clinton used this tour to familiarize herself with issues that mattered to the state's residents.

Those concerns included issues such as health care, education, gun control, and New York's economy. There was something refreshing about a politician who came to listen to the people's concerns rather than just make a speech, shake hands, and then move on to the next town. However, media reaction to the tour was mixed. Some reporters commended Clinton for her decision to learn directly from the electorate, while others, such as *Newsday* reporter Sheryl McCarthy, were less impressed. According to McCarthy, listening "may be a sensible, thoughtful, civilized strategy, but it's also boring."[66]

In September 1999 the Clintons purchased a house in Chappaqua, New York, about 38 miles (61 km) from New York City. It was the first home they had owned in more than twenty years. The one-hundred-year-old Dutch colonial house would serve as the Clintons' post–White House residence and ensure Hillary's compliance with the constitutional requirement that a senator must live in the state that he or she represents.

> *"I think I have some real work to do, to get out and listen and learn from the people of New York and demonstrate that what I'm for is maybe as important, if not more important, than where I'm from."*[63]
>
> —Hillary Clinton.

Clinton's tour took her to New York City, where its mayor, Republican Rudolph Giuliani, was also running for the vacant Senate seat. Polls showed that sometimes Clinton was ahead, and other times Giuliani led. In the spring of 2000, Clinton was ahead when Giuliani, plagued by health issues and marital problems, withdrew from the race. Replacing the mayor as Clinton's Republican opponent was New York congressman Rick Lazio.

Winning the Race

Coming into the race relatively late, Lazio ran a vigorous, mostly negative campaign against Clinton. But neither candidate ran without making blunders. When Clinton, a lifelong Chicago Cubs fan, donned a New York Yankees baseball cap, die-hard Yankee fans chided her for seeming to play politics with their beloved team. She also alienated many Jewish voters by kissing the cheek of Suha Arafat, wife of Palestinian president Yasser Arafat, at a ceremony in Ramallah in the Middle East. Although Suha Arafat had made disparaging remarks about Israel, Clinton explained that the perfunctory kiss was equivalent to a handshake in the Middle East.

Lazio made his own mistake at an event in Buffalo, New York, on September 13, 2000. During a debate between the candidates, Lazio strode toward Clinton's podium carrying a piece of paper concerning campaign funding that he wanted Clinton to sign. Waving the paper in front of Clinton, Lazio stepped closer to her and said, "Right here. Sign it right now. . . . I want your signature!"[67] Lazio's aggressive move into Clinton's personal space backfired, and the incident was enough to destroy his chances for victory, especially among women voters.

On November 7, 2000, Clinton defeated Lazio with 55 percent of the vote. She was New York's first female senator and the only First Lady to be elected to public office. As she later recalled, "After eight years with a title but no portfolio, I was now 'Senator-elect.'"[68]

The Junior Senator from New York

Clinton was sworn in as New York's newest senator (while remaining the First Lady for another two and a half weeks) on January 3, 2001. Her new office was suite SR476 in the Russell Senate Office Building, the same office where Senator Moynihan had worked. She was now the most recognizable senator, but she was also the most junior member of the legislative body. Despite her high public profile, Clinton initially avoided the spotlight and spent her time listening, learning, and familiarizing herself with the issues the Senate was dealing with. She purposely spent time with senators who had disliked the Clintons, even those who had voted to impeach Bill, to prove that she could cooperate with all of her colleagues in order to get legislation passed. According to Jon Corzine, another freshman senator, Clinton said she "wants to be a work horse, not a show horse."[69] Consistent with long-standing practices, Clinton also joined the Senate's Wednesday morning private prayer group.

For the first eight months of her Senate career, Clinton focused on fulfilling her campaign promise to create legislation that would benefit her constituents. This included introducing bills to extend broadband Internet coverage to rural areas, enhancing the State Children's Health

First Daughter on the Campaign Trail

Journalist Beth J. Harpaz was part of the press corps following Hillary Clinton as she ran for the US Senate in 2000. In her book *The Girls in the Van*, she describes how Chelsea Clinton campaigned for her mother.

> The White House announced that Chelsea planned to take off the fall semester of her senior year at Stanford to campaign with her mother and spend time with her father during his last months in office. I took Hillary at her word that this was Chelsea's decision, but it certainly didn't hurt the first lady to have her daughter along. . . .

> On the first day of the Long Island tour, at an outdoor rally in Great Neck, the twenty-year-old first daughter really did seem enthusiastic and had displayed an impressive ability to work the crowd. She hadn't even tried to stay by her mother's side, but instead waded into her own section of the reception line, posing for photographs, shaking hands, signing autographs, leaning down to greet old ladies in wheelchairs and babies in strollers. "Thank you for letting me spend some time with your child," I heard her coo to one parent. She had the perfect posture, clasped hands, and ever-present smile of someone who was accustomed to being stared at, and seemed comfortable accepting the adulation of dozens of gawking strangers who jostled to meet her.

Beth J. Harpaz, *The Girls in the Van.* New York: St. Martin's, 2001, pp. 150–51.

Insurance Program, and creating grants to improve job skills for those seeking employment in certain industries. Clinton also served on the Senate Committee on the Budget, the Senate Committee on the Environment and Public Works, and the Senate Committee on Health, Education, Labor and Pensions. Clinton kept her low profile, sponsoring legislation and becoming comfortable with the workings of the Senate. Then, on September 11, 2001, the world changed.

Terrorists Strike New York

Clinton was about to leave her house on Whitehaven Street in Washington, DC, for her morning ride to Capitol Hill when she heard that an airplane had flown into the North Tower of New York's World Trade Center. Like many people that morning, Clinton at first believed the crash was simply a tragic accident. But as she rode to her scheduled meeting on the Hill, a radio report told of another plane crashing into the World Trade Center's South Tower. It soon became clear that the planes had been hijacked by terrorists who used them as weapons to attack the United States.

Chelsea Clinton lived and worked in New York City, so Clinton naturally became concerned about her twenty-one-year-old daughter's safety. After failing to reach Chelsea's cell phone, Clinton called her husband, who was in Australia for a speech. Not wanting to alarm Bill but unsure of Chelsea's whereabouts, she merely told him, "Everything's fine. Don't worry."[70] Hillary eventually spoke to Chelsea, breathing a sigh of relief when she learned that her daughter was safe.

In less than two hours after the first crash, the World Trade Center's Twin Towers had collapsed into a smoking pile of rubble.

> "That September morning changed me, and what I had to do as a Senator, a New Yorker and an American."[71]
>
> —Hillary Clinton.

After a third airliner crashed into the Pentagon just outside of Washington, radar showed a fourth plane changing course and heading eastward. Officials assumed that Washington was the plane's target, so Clinton and her Senate colleagues who worked in various office buildings were evacuated to safer quarters. That plane never reached its destination, because the brave passengers on board breached the cockpit and forced the aircraft into a deadly dive, crashing it into a Pennsylvania field. In all, nearly three thousand people perished in the September 11 terrorist attacks. "That September morning changed me," Clinton wrote in her autobiography, "and what I had to do as a Senator, a New Yorker and an American."[71]

Senator Hillary Clinton joins New York City mayor Rudolph Giuliani and other dignitaries on a tour of the ruins of the World Trade Center on September 12, 2001. New York's two senators requested—and received—$20 billion in federal aid for the city.

9/11 Aftermath

The day after the terrorist attacks, Clinton toured Ground Zero with Mayor Giuliani and officials from the New York City fire and police departments. Rescue workers were digging through the rubble of the two ruined towers as gray smoke rose into the sky from the fires that still burned. After returning to Washington, Clinton and fellow New York senator Charles Schumer met with President George W. Bush to request $20 billion in federal aid for New York City. The president replied, "You've got it."[72]

The September 11 attacks caused more damage apart from the initial destruction of the Twin Towers. Smoke, ash, and pulverized debris contaminated the air over Lower Manhattan, where the World Trade Center had been located. Toxic fumes and dust caused severe respiratory problems for thousands of first responders, construction workers, and volunteers at Ground Zero. Clinton pushed for further research on the air quality at Ground Zero and improved health care for 9/11 first responders.

> *"This is a very difficult vote. This is probably the hardest decision I have ever had to make—any vote that may lead to war should be hard—but I cast it with conviction."* [75]
>
> —Hillary Clinton.

Despite Clinton's efforts in the weeks after 9/11, some New Yorkers still harbored resentment against her. On October 20 a benefit concert organized by singer Paul McCartney was held at Madison Square Garden to raise funds for the victims of 9/11. As she walked onstage, Clinton was booed by many members of the audience, which included New York police officers and firefighters. It was a highly emotional night, and the first responders were not inclined to show approval of a politician not supported by their union. Clinton later played down the incident, calling it "part of the healing process." [73]

A Nation at War

On the evening of the attacks, Bush addressed the American people on television. "The search is underway for those who are behind these evil acts," he said, sitting behind his desk in the Oval Office. "I've directed the full resources of our intelligence and law enforcement communities to find those responsible and to bring them to justice." [74] Evidence pointed to the terrorist organization al Qaeda, led by Osama bin Laden, as the group behind the attacks. When the United States invaded Afghanistan, where al Qaeda's headquarters and training camps were located, Clinton joined most of her congressional colleagues in supporting this action—the first phase of America's War on Terror. She also voted in favor of the USA Patriot Act, which gave law enforcement agencies increased power to conduct surveillance and gather intelligence to help prevent future acts of terrorism against the United States.

In 2002 Bush expanded the War on Terror, launching an attack against Iraq and its dictator, Saddam Hussein. Clinton voted in favor of the invasion, called Operation Iraqi Freedom. Speaking to the Senate on the day of the vote, Clinton said, "This is a very difficult vote. This is probably the hardest decision I have ever had to make—any vote that may lead to war should be hard—but I cast it with conviction."[75]

A Regretted Vote

Sometimes one moment can have a lasting effect, for good or ill, on a person. For Senator Hillary Clinton, that moment was her vote to support the war in Iraq initiated by President George W. Bush. In her book *Hard Choices*, Clinton recalls the backlash from her vote.

> Wherever I traveled I heard from people who were dead set against the war and, as a result, personally disappointed in me. Many had been opposed from the start; others turned against it over time. Hardest of all were the anguished military families who wanted their loved ones to come home, veterans worried about their buddies still serving tours in Iraq, and Americans of all walks of life who were heartbroken by the losses of our young men and women. . . .
>
> While many were never going to look past my 2002 vote no matter what I did or said, I should have stated my regret sooner and in the plainest, most direct language possible. . . . I thought I had acted in good faith and made the best decision I could with the information I had. And I wasn't alone in getting it wrong. But I still got it wrong. Plain and simple.

Hillary Rodham Clinton, *Hard Choices*. New York: Simon & Schuster, 2014, pp. 136–37.

A US soldier patrols in Iraq in 2008. When President George W. Bush asked Congress to approve the use of force in Iraq in 2002, Clinton was among those who voted in favor of the invasion.

Predictions of a quick end to the war soon proved erroneous. Clinton's record of supporting Bush's military operations began to change as the Iraq War dragged on and the cost of the conflict continued to rise. On *The Today Show* in 2006, Clinton said, "Obviously, if we knew then what we know now, there wouldn't have been a vote and I certainly wouldn't have voted that way."[76] Since that television appearance, Clinton has been asked many times if she felt her vote on Iraq was wrong. She now says that Congress made a bad decision, but she has never used the word *mistake* in referring to her own vote.

Senator and Author

Clinton won reelection to the Senate in November 2006, garnering more than twice the number of votes than her opponent received. By her second term Clinton had become a member of the Senate's powerful Armed Services Committee, which oversees the affairs of the nation's military. It was a rare honor not usually given to a senator so early in his or her Senate career. As part of the committee, Clinton learned about weapons and military strategy, information that would help her in her future political life. By this time Clinton's support of the war had changed, and she voted against a proposed troop surge in Iraq in 2007. She also opposed a new war funding bill in May 2007, but it nevertheless became law.

Clinton's public profile and her influence as a senator rose during her second term. She promoted legislation concerning children's health, the environment, education, and the struggling US economy. One of Clinton's strengths was her ability to work with Senate Republicans in order to drive legislation that was important to her. She collaborated with many senators "across the aisle," including forging an alliance with Lindsey Graham on a bill to broaden veterans' health benefits to include members of the National Guard and military reserves. Along with Senate Majority Leader Bill Frist, Clinton pushed for the establishment of electronic medical records. She also worked with the Republican former Speaker of the House of Representatives, Newt Gingrich, on important national issues. "The speaker and I have been talking about health care and national security now for several years," Clinton noted, "and I find that he and I have a lot in common in the way we see the problem." Gingrich characterized Clinton as "very smart and very hard working."[77] Clinton was able to overlook the fact that Gingrich had been one of the strongest advocates for Bill Clinton's impeachment.

During her two terms as a senator, Clinton sponsored or cosponsored 3,387 bills, 77 of which became law. She also had another accomplishment to add to her résumé: a second best-selling book. In June 2003 Clinton's autobiography, *Living History*, was published. The book chronicles Clinton's life from growing up in Park Ridge to her years as First Lady of the United States. *Living History* became immensely popular, selling some six hundred thousand copies during its first week in bookstores and ultimately being translated into numerous foreign languages. *Living History* did have its detractors, however. One journalist criticized Clinton for her mostly gentle portrayal of her abusive father and for downplaying her marital difficulties. Many critics felt that with *Living History*, Clinton was simply setting the stage for her next political objective: a run for the presidency of the United States.

Chapter Five

Running for the White House

On January 20, 2007—two years to the day before America's next chief executive would be sworn in—Clinton declared her intention to run for president. She sent an e-mail to her supporters, beginning with, "I'm in. And I'm in to win,"[78] announcing the formation of a presidential exploratory committee. In a short video on her Hillary for President website, Clinton sat on a couch in her Washington, DC, home, appearing relaxed and friendly. She spoke plainly to the people whose vote she hoped to win.

> You know, after six years of George Bush, it is time to renew the promise of America. Our basic bargain that no matter who you are or where you live, if you work hard and play by the rules, you can build a good life for yourself and your family.
>
> I grew up in a middle-class family in the middle of America, and we believed in that promise. I still do. I've spent my entire life trying to make good on it. Whether it was fighting for women's basic rights or children's basic health care. Protecting our Social Security, or protecting our soldiers. It's a kind of basic bargain, and we've got to keep up our end.
>
> So let the conversation begin. I have a feeling it's going to be very interesting.[79]

The conversation between Clinton and the American people was a series of live, online chats begun the Monday after her announcement. The interactive chats, where people typed in questions and Clinton responded, became a high-tech listening tour. Over three nights questions touched on topics ranging from terrorism, the environment, and health care to such personal matters as what Clinton did when she was not working. As with her 1999 Senate campaign listening tour, Clinton's chats had their critics. Some said that the chats were prearranged and staged so Clinton could avoid dealing with difficult questions she might be unprepared to answer. But Clinton ignored these critics as she prepared for the tough campaign ahead.

Seeking Voters

Clinton was not alone on the campaign trail. Seven other Democrats were pursuing the nomination, but the two most credible opponents were Illinois senator Barack Obama and former South Carolina senator John Edwards. Clinton's high profile as a former First Lady and current senator gave her the lead over the other candidates in early polls. Yet not everyone welcomed the idea of another Clinton in the White House, and her initial stand supporting the Iraq War was seen as troubling by many voters.

> *"I'm in. And I'm in to win."*[78]
>
> —Hillary Clinton.

Clinton spent much of 2007 raising campaign funds and talking to voters. She retained a commanding lead in the national polls. But beneath the confident exterior, her campaign was slowly falling into disarray as the different personalities of the Clinton staff clashed. By July, Obama was making inroads into Clinton's popularity. Despite her experience being in front of crowds, Clinton's speaking technique often made her look cold and unsympathetic—the opposite of Obama's upbeat, likeable style. In order to bring that same spirit to her campaign, Clinton tapped a reliable source: her husband.

At a rally at the Iowa State Fairgrounds in Des Moines on July 2, a smiling Bill introduced Hillary to the crowd. During her speech he sat quietly onstage on a low stool, not wanting to draw attention to himself. As she took the microphone, Hillary spoke to a receptive crowd that frequently cheered and applauded. She said: "I am very proud to be running as a woman to make history as our first woman president. That is exciting. But I am not running as a woman. I am running because I believe I am the best qualified and experienced

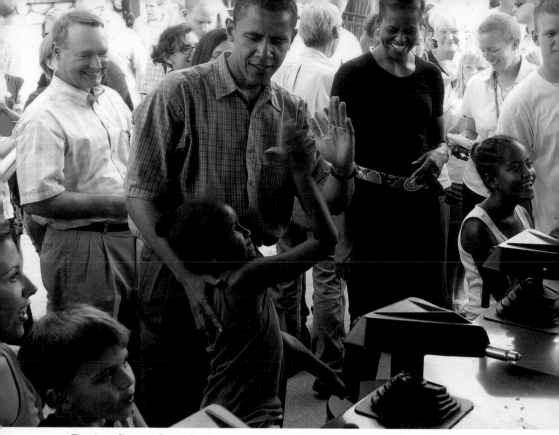

During the presidential primary campaign, Democratic hopeful Barack Obama (shown in Iowa in 2007) demonstrated an upbeat, likeable style. At the same time, some criticized Hillary Clinton for coming across as cold and unsympathetic.

person to hit the ground running to do the work that we need to do starting in 2009."[80] Throughout the next months the Clintons traveled throughout Iowa—visiting schools, attending picnics and barbecues, and speaking to countless voters and veterans' groups, senior citizens, and union leaders.

Disaster in Iowa

The first major test for Clinton and her campaign team came in January 2008, as Iowa voters flocked to caucus sites to choose the Democratic presidential candidate. As the night wore on, it became apparent that polls predicting a Clinton victory had missed their mark. Obama had won in Iowa. The final tally showed Clinton in third place, slightly behind Edwards and trailing Obama by a wide margin. After spending more than $20 million campaigning in Iowa, Clinton had come up short.

The next contest, in New Hampshire, was only five days away. As Clinton and her campaign team headed north, they discussed what strategies they could use to slow Obama's momentum. Winning the New Hampshire vote was critical: If she lost there, her staff believed, her bid for president would be all but over.

Primary Season

Based on his win in Iowa, Obama led the polls in New Hampshire going into that state's primary. For the first time Clinton was not the front-runner, and she only had a few days to connect with the voters of the Granite State. She made the most of that time, holding informal meetings in hopes of swaying the undecided. In a coffee shop in Portsmouth, Clinton was talking to a group of sixteen voters when she suddenly showed her vulnerable side. Answering a question about how she managed to "get out the door every day" during a tough campaign, Clinton gave a glib response, but then suddenly turned serious. As tears welled in her eyes and her voice quivered, she quietly said, "You know, this is very personal for me. It's not just political, it's not just public. I see what's happening. . . . I just believe so strongly in who we are as a nation. So I'm going to do everything I can to make my case, and then the voters get to decide."[81]

New Hampshire voters chose Clinton as their Democratic nominee. Clinton won 39 percent of the votes, followed by Obama with 36 percent and Edwards with 17 percent. It was a stunning victory for Clinton. Her campaign advisers hoped that the momentum from New Hampshire would propel her to victory in a number of races scheduled for February 5.

Super Tuesday and Beyond

Tuesday, February 5, 2008, was called Super Tuesday because Democratic primaries and caucuses were scheduled in twenty-two states representing more than half of the votes needed for the nomination. The only two viable Democratic candidates remaining at this point were Clinton and Obama. The differences between the two candidates created a thought-provoking choice for voters. Clinton was a Washington insider who had traveled extensively and met with world

Losing Iowa

Hillary's stunning loss in the Iowa caucuses threw her campaign into a tailspin of depression. The mood at Clinton headquarters was grim, as journalists John Heilemann and Mark Halperin describe the scene.

> The next four hours were a blur for Hillary Clinton. Reeling from the loss, she appeared onstage for a televised speech surrounded by old and pale faces—Madeleine Albright, Wesley Clark, her husband—that created an unflattering contrast with the young and multiracial tableau presented by Obama. Back upstairs at the hotel, she had to be coaxed into thanking her Iowa staff and major fund-raisers, who were gathered in a nearby suite. "Yeah, okay," she said. Standing on a chair, steadied by [campaign chair Terry] McAuliffe, she told the crowd that everything would be all right. It was just one loss, the race ahead would be long; she was on to New Hampshire. But the expression on her face belied her words: with her frozen smile, her dazed eyes, she looked as if she were having an out-of-body experience.

John Heilemann and Mark Halperin, *Game Change: Obama and the Clintons, McCain and Palin, and the Race of a Lifetime*. New York: Harper, 2010, p. 173.

leaders. Although she was a familiar figure to the American people, many considered her cold and aloof. Obama, a relative newcomer to the Washington scene, had spent only two years as a US senator and had no prior national political experience. But he came across as young, energetic, and warm—a fresh candidate who was the bearer of hope for the future.

When the Super Tuesday votes were counted, Obama had won thirteen of the twenty-two state contests to Clinton's nine. Obama's campaign was starting to pick up speed, while Clinton's comeback was on the verge of stalling. More primaries were scheduled to be held over the next several months. Clinton, who had envisioned a quick victory after her New Hampshire win, was not prepared for an extended campaign and was running low on funds. In January she had loaned the campaign $5 million of her own money to keep it afloat. The Clinton campaign continued to work hard to raise more money. But as Clinton piled up wins in Pennsylvania, Ohio, and Indiana, Obama won in Wisconsin, Virginia, and Hawaii. By the time the June 3 primaries in Montana and South Carolina were over, Obama had gained enough delegates to be declared the winner of the Democratic nomination for president.

Accepting Defeat

Although Obama had enough delegates to win the nomination, Clinton did not immediately admit defeat. One of her advisers noted, "She could accept losing. She could not accept quitting."[82] Clinton still held out hope that Democratic superdelegates, important party leaders who can vote for any candidate they choose, could still turn the tide in her favor. But it was not to be. On June 7 Clinton conceded the nomination, thanking her supporters and pledging her support to her former opponent.

Clinton had mounted a historic campaign, amassing more than 18 million primary votes. When she returned to the Senate on June 24, she was warmly received by her colleagues on the Senate floor. She was ready to serve out her interrupted term and continue creating legislation for health care and the economy. But the future held an even more important job for the woman who had come closer to the presidency than any before her.

> "She could accept losing. She could not accept quitting."[82]
>
> —A Clinton campaign adviser.

A New Era in Diplomacy

On November 4, 2008, Democrat Barack Obama beat Republican John McCain in the race for president. The excitement surrounding the election of America's first African American president had hardly subsided when the rumors began to circulate that president-elect Obama would offer Clinton a job in his administration. Clinton's initial reaction to the rumors was unambiguous. "I was not interested in serving in the Cabinet. I wanted to go back to the Senate and my work for New York."[83] But Obama had other ideas for his former rival. On November 13 he asked Clinton to be his secretary of state, saying that he felt she was the only person for the job. After a week of considering her options and consulting with her advisers and family, Clinton accepted the post.

After Obama was elected president, he asked Clinton to serve as secretary of state. She traveled extensively in that role. She is shown here during a 2011 visit to Tanzania in Africa.

January 22, 2009, was Clinton's first day on the job as secretary of state. In a scene reminiscent of her campaign appearances, Clinton entered the US Department of State building to the applause and cheers of her new colleagues. "I believe with all my heart," she told the crowd, "that this is a new era for America."[84] Clinton spent the first week of her job phoning dozens of world leaders to discuss issues of mutual importance, a goodwill gesture to assure them that America was taking a new direction in foreign policy after the Bush years.

World Traveler

As First Lady, Clinton had traveled the world on behalf of her husband's administration, gaining knowledge of other cultures and meeting diplomats and ordinary people. Now such travel was the purpose of her job as secretary of state. Traditionally, newly appointed secretaries of state make their first overseas visits to Europe, home to many of America's strongest allies. But Clinton decided to make Asia her first destination, flying to Tokyo on February 15 to kick off a visit to Japan, China, Indonesia, and South Korea. On the seven-day whirlwind tour, Clinton met with foreign ministers and ordinary citizens, holding town hall meetings to learn the views of the people. Her discussion topics ranged from the world's economy and global warming to North Korea's nuclear aspirations and women's rights. The Asian tour was a grueling trek of late-night flights and overcrowded schedules. One of the journalists that accompanied Clinton lamented, "If every one of her trips is going to be run like a campaign stop, we're all going to fall apart."[85]

Clinton next visited the Middle East and Europe. Her subsequent trips spanned the globe from Latin America to Africa and from Russia to Australia. During her tenure as secretary of state, Clinton visited 112 countries and traveled 956,733 miles (1.5 million km), making her the most-traveled secretary of state in US history.

February 1, 2013, was Clinton's last day as secretary of state. After she left office, commentators assessed her four years as America's chief diplomat. Many said that she was merely adequate at her job, never signing any major treaties or brokering peace between unfriendly nations. Some considered her tenure simply a stepping stone to another run for president. David Gordon, who had worked in the State

Department under George W. Bush, characterized Clinton as a "good not great" secretary of state, whose "great weakness was avoiding serious diplomacy."[86] But among her accomplishments were rebuilding America's stature in the eyes of the world and acknowledging Asia as a critical focus for American diplomacy. Anne-Marie Slaughter, Clinton's former director of policy planning, notes, "I continue to think that people will look back and see that she was the first secretary of state really to grasp the ways global politics and hence foreign policy have changed in the 21st century."[87]

Another Run

During her term as secretary of state, Clinton met rumors of the possibility of another presidential campaign with denials. But her years at the State Department had increased her stature as someone who could handle foreign affairs with dignity and intelligence and had boosted her public approval rating to 70 percent. Clinton decided to once more hit the campaign trail.

On April 12, 2015, Clinton announced her intention to run for president via a YouTube video showing ordinary Americans planning for their futures, and Clinton vowing to help people like them succeed if she was elected.

Clinton's first campaign event was her formal kickoff rally on June 15 at New York City's Roosevelt Island. "I'm running to make our economy work for you and for every American," she told the crowd of about five thousand supporters. "I may not be the youngest candidate in this race. But I will be the youngest woman president in the history of the United States."[88]

> "I continue to think that people will look back and see that she was the first secretary of state really to grasp the ways global politics and hence foreign policy have changed in the 21st century."[87]
>
> —Anne-Marie Slaughter, Clinton's former director of policy planning.

Donations and E-mails

Controversy had followed Clinton throughout her career, and the 2016 presidential campaign was no exception. When she announced

Benghazi

On September 11, 2012, terrorists attacked the US diplomatic compound in Benghazi, Libya, killing four Americans, including US ambassador J. Christopher Stevens. The fifty-two-year-old Stevens, whose career included posts throughout the Middle East, had been sent to Libya by Secretary of State Hillary Clinton in April 2011.

The death of such a high-ranking US diplomat assured that the incident would receive intense scrutiny by US officials. Five committees in the Republican-led House of Representatives immediately launched inquiries into the attack. They investigated rumors of conspiracies, illegal arms deals, and delays in sending rescuers to the compound. In January 2013 Clinton testified for five hours before Congress to answer questions about Benghazi, saying that, as secretary of state, she bore responsibility for the tragedy. An interim report issued in April 2013 criticized security at the Benghazi compound and claimed that the Obama administration made misleading statements regarding the cause of the attack. House Democrats complained that the committees, led by Republicans, were unfairly biased in their investigations. Over the next year, more congressional inquiries on the attack were held. In November 2014 the House Intelligence Committee, one of the original five investigating bodies, released its final report. It concluded that there was no evidence of wrongdoing or conspiracy concerning the Benghazi attack.

In her testimony before Congress, Clinton demonstrated toughness and candor in dealing with difficult questions in an emotionally charged situation. These qualities would be vital in her run for president in 2016.

her candidacy, questions immediately arose concerning money donated to the Bill, Hillary & Chelsea Clinton Foundation, as well as speaking fees paid to the Clintons. Many observers expressed concern that the corporate and foreign donors might seek special favors as a reward for their donations if Hillary won the election. Although such

After announcing her intention to seek the Democratic nomination for president, Hillary Clinton speaks to supporters at 2015 rally in New York. Clinton hopes to be the first woman president in US history.

donations were legal, they became a point of contention as Clinton's campaign got underway.

Another controversy concerned e-mails Clinton had sent during her term as secretary of state. While conducting State Department business, Clinton set up a personal account and used a private e-mail server located in her Chappaqua, New York, home. Federal law states that all government employees must use official e-mail accounts and save all official e-mails. Clinton's aides countered that her use of a private server did not violate State Department regulations and that former secretaries of state had done the same thing.

Clinton stated in a press conference that about half of her sixty thousand e-mails were personal in nature and had been deleted by her staff, while the rest, containing official business, were turned over to the State Department. After months of steadfastly refusing to apologize for using a private e-mail account, Clinton finally did so in a television interview on September 8. "That was a mistake," she told ABC's David Muir. "I'm sorry about that."[89] Despite these controversies, Clinton remained the front-runner and most popular of the Democratic candidates, and the possibility of a woman president appeared closer than ever.

Hillary Clinton has achieved many milestones in her life, from being the first woman commencement speaker at Wellesley to becoming the most-traveled US secretary of state. Her 2008 presidential bid failed, but failure has never kept Clinton down for long. If her nomination as the Democratic candidate for president succeeds, she will be the first woman presidential candidate of a major party. If she is elected, she will have reached the ultimate milestone as America's first woman president. She has endured personal and political crises and remained a strong, if polarizing, figure in American politics. Ultimately, it will be up to history to judge the life and accomplishments of this influential woman.

Source Notes

Introduction: The Many Lives of Hillary Clinton

1. Quoted in Norman King, *The Woman in the White House: The Remarkable Story of Hillary Rodham Clinton*. New York: Birch Lane, 1996, p. 5.

2. Quoted in Matthew T. Corrigan, *American Royalty: The Bush and Clinton Families and the Danger to the American Presidency*. New York: Palgrave Macmillan, 2008, p. 11.

3. Quoted in Amy Chozik, "Hillary Clinton Announces 2016 Presidential Bid," *New York Times*, April 12, 2015. www.nytimes.com.

Chapter One: Hillary Growing Up

4. Quoted in Donnie Radcliffe, *Hillary Rodham Clinton: A First Lady for Our Time*. New York: Warner, 1993, p. 42.

5. Quoted in Radcliffe, *Hillary Rodham Clinton*, pp. 30–31.

6. Quoted in Hillary Rodham Clinton, *Living History*. New York: Simon & Schuster, 2003, p. 12.

7. Quoted in Carl Bernstein, *A Woman in Charge: The Life of Hillary Rodham Clinton*. New York: Knopf, 2007, p. 20.

8. Quoted in Joyce Milton, *The First Partner, Hillary Rodham Clinton*. New York: Morrow, 1999, p. 13.

9. Clinton, *Living History*, p. 11.

10. Quoted in Matt Hickman, "10 Famous Former Girl Scouts," Mother Nature Network, February 19, 2013. www.mnn.com.

11. Quoted in King, *The Woman in the White House*, p. 11.

12. Quoted in Cynthia Hanson, "I Was a Teenage Republican," *Chicago*, September 1994. www.chicagomag.com.

13. Hillary Rodham Clinton, *It Takes a Village*. New York: Simon & Schuster, 1996, p. 171.

14. Clinton, *Living History*, pp. 22–23.

15. Clinton, *Living History*, p. 23.

16. Clinton, *Living History*, p. 11.

17. Clinton, *Living History*, p. 17.

18. Clinton, *Living History*, p. 20.

19. Clinton, *Living History*, p. 24.

20. Quoted in Christianity.com, "John Wesley," 2015. www.christian ity.com.

Chapter Two: Wellesley, Yale, and Bill Clinton

21. Quoted in Bernstein, *A Woman in Charge*, p. 41.

22. Clinton, *Living History*, p. 27.

23. Clinton, *Living History*, pp. 27–28.

24. Quoted in King, *The Woman in the White House*, p. 15.

25. Quoted in King, *The Woman in the White House*, p. 15.

26. Quoted in Paul Kengor, *God and Hillary Clinton: A Spiritual Life*. New York: HarperCollins, 2007, p. 28.

27. Quoted in Howard G. Chua-Eoan, "Power Mom," *People*, January 25, 1993, p. 58.

28. Quoted in Bernstein, *A Woman in Charge*, p. 50.

29. Quoted in Radcliffe, *Hillary Rodham Clinton*, p. 68.

30. Clinton, *Living History*, p. 33.

31. Quoted in Radcliffe, *Hillary Rodham Clinton*, p. 69.

32. Quoted in Bernstein, *A Woman in Charge*, p. 54.

33. Clinton, *Living History*, p. 36.

34. Quoted in Radcliffe, *Hillary Rodham Clinton*, p. 75.

35. Quoted in Gail Sheehy, *Hillary's Choice*. New York: Random House, 1999, p. 86.

36. Clinton, *Living History*, p. 40.

37. Quoted in Bernstein, *A Woman in Charge*, p. 58.

38. Quoted in Miriam Horn, *Rebels in White Gloves: Coming of Age with Hillary's Class—Wellesley '69*. New York: Times, 1999, p. 47.

39. Quoted in Radcliffe, *Hillary Rodham Clinton*, p. 89.

40. Clinton, *Living History*, p. 52.

41. William H. Chafe, *Bill and Hillary: The Politics of the Personal*. New York: Farrar, Straus and Giroux, 2012, p. 72.

42. Quoted in Sheehy, *Hillary's Choice*, p. 82.

Chapter Three: First Lady Hillary

43. Quoted in Bill Clinton, *My Life*. New York: Knopf, 2004, p. 69.

44. Clinton, *My Life*, p. 228.

45. Clinton, *My Life*, p. 233.

46. Quoted in Bernstein, *A Woman in Charge*, p. 130.

47. Bernstein, *A Woman in Charge*, p. 140.

48. Quoted in Bernstein, *A Woman in Charge*, p. 123.

49. Chafe, *Bill and Hillary*, p. 112.

50. Quoted in Christopher Anderson, *Bill and Hillary: The Marriage*. New York: Morrow, 1999, p. 182.

51. Quoted in Sheehy, *Hillary's Choice*, p. 208.

52. Clinton, *Living History*, p. 102.

53. Clinton, *Living History*, p. 107.

54. Clinton, *Living History*, p. 109.

55. Bernstein, *A Woman in Charge*, p. 284.

56. Quoted in Judy Keen and Mimi Hall, "Leading the Crusade: First Lady Takes Role as Saleswoman," *USA Today*, September 28, 1993, p. 1A.

57. Clinton, *Living History*, p. 248.

58. Quoted in Brooks Jackson, "Giving Hillary Credit for SCHIP," FactCheck.org, March 18, 2008. www.factcheck.org.

59. Bill Clinton, "Response to the Lewinsky Allegations (January 26, 1998)," Miller Center, University of Virginia, 2015. www.miller center.org.

60. Clinton, *Living History*, p. 445.

61. Clinton, *Living History*, p. 527.

Chapter Four: Senator Clinton

62. Clinton, *Living History*, p. 483.

63. Quoted in Andrew D. Wolvin, "Listening Leadership: Hillary Clinton's Listening Tour," *International Journal of Listening*, 2005. http://3rdyearwiki0809.pbworks.com.

64. Quoted in Jeff Gerth and Don Van Natta Jr., *Her Way: The Hopes and Ambitions of Hillary Rodham Clinton*. New York: Little, Brown, 2007, p. 209.

65. Clinton, *Living History*, p. 511.

66. Quoted in Wolvin, "Listening Leadership."

67. C-SPAN Video, "First Debate Clinton-Lazio, 2000—Part 6." www.youtube.com/watch?v=YMJZo4UeTYQ.

68. Clinton, *Living History*, p. 524.

69. Quoted in Mary Jacoby, "Hillary Clinton Suits Up for Senate Team," *St. Petersburg (FL) Times*, December 6, 2000. www.sptimes.com.

70. Quoted in Gerth and Van Natta, *Her Way*, p. 227.

71. Clinton, *Living History*, p. xi.

72. Quoted in Gerth and Van Natta, *Her Way*, p. 231.

73. Quoted in Gerth and Van Natta, *Her Way*, p. 237.

74. George W. Bush, "Address to the Nation on the September 11 Attacks," *Selected Speeches of President George W. Bush, 2001–2008*, White House, p. 65. http://georgewbush-whitehouse.archives.gov.

75. Quoted in Bernstein, *A Woman in Charge*, p. 549.

76. Quoted in ABC News, "Hillary Clinton Says She Wouldn't Have Voted for Iraq War," December 29, 2006. www.abcnews.com.

77. Quoted in Raymond Hernandez, "Oddly, Hillary and, Yes, Newt Agree to Agree," *New York Times*, May 13, 2005. www.nytimes.com.

Chapter Five: Running for the White House

78. Hillary Clinton, "Presidential Exploratory Committee Announcement," video transcript, January 20, 2007. www.4president.us.

79. Clinton, "Presidential Exploratory Committee Announcement."

80. Hillary Clinton, "Clinton Campaign Event," video transcript, C-SPAN, July 2, 2007. www.c-span.org.

81. Hillary Clinton, "Hillary Tears Up in New Hampshire Primary 2008," video, YouTube. www.youtube.com.

82. Quoted in Dan Balz and Haynes Johnson, *The Battle for America 2008: The Story of an Extraordinary Election*. New York: Viking, 2009, p. 216.

83. Hillary Rodham Clinton, *Hard Choices*. New York: Simon & Schuster, 2014, p. 13.

84. Quoted in Kim Ghattas, *The Secretary: A Journey with Hillary Clinton from Beirut to the Heart of American Power*. New York: Times, 2013, p. 13.

85. Quoted in Ghattas, *The Secretary*, p. 50.

86. Quoted in Susan B. Glasser, "Was Hillary Clinton a Good Secretary of State?," *Politico*, December 8, 2013. www.politico.com.

87. Quoted in Glasser, "Was Hillary Clinton a Good Secretary of State?"

88. Quoted in *Time*, "Read the Full Text of Hillary Clinton's Campaign Launch Speech," transcript, June 13, 2015. www.time.com.

89. Quoted in Anne Gearan, "Hillary Clinton Apologizes for E-Mail System: 'I Take Responsibility.'" *Washington Post*, September 8, 2015. www.washingtonpost.com.

Important Events in the Life of Hillary Clinton

1947

Hillary Rodham is born on October 26 in Chicago, Illinois.

1962

With her church youth group, Hillary attends a speech given by Martin Luther King Jr. in Chicago; she is inspired by King's words.

1965

Hillary enters Wellesley College in Massachusetts.

1969

Wellesley invites its student body president, Hillary Rodham, to give a commencement address—a first for the college.

1971

Hillary Rodham meets fellow Yale Law School student Bill Clinton.

1975

The couple marries in Little Rock, Arkansas.

1976

Clinton joins the prestigious Rose Law Firm.

1980

Daughter Chelsea Victoria Clinton is born on February 27.

1983

Clinton is appointed head of the Arkansas Education Standards Committee.

1992

Bill Clinton is elected forty-second president of the United States, with Hillary as his First Lady.

2000

Clinton defeats Rick Lazio to become US senator from New York.

2002

Clinton joins most of her Senate colleagues in granting President George W. Bush's request for authorization to use force against Iraq.

2003

Clinton's memoir, *Living History*, is published.

2007

Clinton announces her candidacy for president of the United States.

2008

Barack Obama defeats Clinton in the Democratic primaries and caucuses and goes on to win election as president against the Republican challenger, John McCain.

2010

Clinton is sworn in as US secretary of state.

2013

Clinton testifies before the Senate regarding the terrorist attacks in Benghazi, Libya.

2015

Clinton announces that she is seeking the Democratic nomination for president; she begins campaigning with an eye toward the November 2016 presidential election.

For Further Research

Books

Jonathan Allen and Amie Parnes, *HRC: The State Secrets and Rebirth of Hillary Clinton*. New York: Crown, 2014.

William H. Chafe, *Bill and Hillary: The Politics of the Personal*. New York: Farrar, Straus and Giroux, 2012.

Hillary Rodham Clinton, *Living History*. New York: Simon & Schuster, 2003.

Hillary Rodham Clinton, *Hard Choices*. New York: Simon & Schuster, 2014.

Kim Ghattas, *The Secretary: A Journey with Hillary Clinton from Beirut to the Heart of American Power*. New York: Times, 2013.

Lisa Rogak, ed., *Hillary Clinton in Her Own Words*. Berkeley, CA: Seal, 2014.

Internet Sources

Andrea Bernstein, "Is Hillary Clinton Really a New Yorker?," *National Public Radio*, June 12, 2015. www.npr.org/sections/itsallpolitics/2015/06/12/413974704/is-hillary-clinton-a-new-yorker.

Sam Frizzell, "Hillary Clinton Continues Listening Tour in New Hampshire," *Time*, April 20, 2015. http://time.com/3828914/hillary-clinton-listening-tour/.

Susan B. Glasser, "Was Hillary Clinton a Good Secretary of State?," *Politico*, December 8, 2013. www.politico.com/magazine/story/2013|/12/was-hillary-clinton-a-good-secretary-of-state-john-kerry-2016-100766.html#.VaAJ5_mUKCg.

Dan Merica, "From Park Ridge to Washington: The Youth Minister Who Mentored Hillary Clinton," CNN, April 25, 2014. www.cnn.com/2014/04/25/politics/clinton-methodist-minister.

Becca Stanek, "Hillary Clinton as Senator of New York Boasted a List of Significant Achievements," *Bustle.com*. www.bustle.com/articles/83420-hillary-clinton-as-senator-of-new-york-boasted-a-list-of-significant-achievements.

Websites

4president (www.4president.us). This website chronicles presidential campaigns from 1960 through 2016. Includes candidate websites, TV ads, and links to blogs and Twitter.

Hillary for America (www.hillaryclinton.com). This is the official website for Hillary Clinton's 2016 presidential campaign.

National First Ladies' Library (www.firstladies.org). Includes biographies of all of America's first ladies, plus a historical timeline, First Lady trivia, news articles, and an informative blog.

US Department of State (www.state.gov). An in-depth government website with information on US foreign policy, international diplomacy, nations of the world, and current and former secretaries of state.

White House (www.whitehouse.gov). The official White House website presents a wealth of information about the executive mansion, its history, current and previous occupants, plus an interactive tour.

Index

Picture Credits

About the Author

Craig E. Blohm has written numerous books and magazine articles for young readers. He and his wife, Desiree, reside in Tinley Park, Illinois.